One Step At A Time

A Motivational Conversation

Tanya R. Hellams

One Step At A Time

One Step At A Time

A Motivational Conversation

Tanya R. Hellams

Kindle Direct Publishing

One Step At A Time

Publishers Information

No part of this book may be reproduced or transmitted in any form or means, electronic or mechanical, including photocopying, recording or by any information storage and retrieval system without permission in writing from the publisher except in the case of brief quotations embodied in critical articles and reviews.

ISBM: 979-8-218-53133-1

Independently published

Book Cover Illustrations designed by Asya Sheley

Printed in the United States of America

November 2024

Preface

This inspiring work of art comes from a place of true desire for you to rest in your best place, your happy place. The author always wants you to be the best version of you for yourself first and then to others. The words are meant to be a conversation between old friends. With that, as you read the words that drive her passion, there may be some action required to place the task into practice which may require a shift in your way of thinking and a change to your outward/inward behaviors.

Any situation is all about your perspective. It takes great courage to take a step forward when you have been pushed backwards time and time again. At some point, we become afraid to move, to ask, or to think we can.

One Step At A Time

Let's put your thoughts and actions in a different perspective or view it from a different angle, one step at a time. Remember, you can because you tried.

"You don't have to have it all figured out to move forward. Just take the next step."

Anonymous

Dedication

I would like to dedicate this inspiring work to those who had no idea, or maybe they did have an idea that their words would have such an impact on my life; this work of art comes from a place of what I have been told and personally experienced.

Acknowledgment

I want to thank my dad, Clyde Meeks, who always believed in me and pushed me past my self-imposed limitations, I did it! Thank you to my mom, Jacqueline Nightingale, who pushed me to do better than yesterday and my grandmother, Bernice Buford, who was there every day.

I want to thank the crew that encouraged me to put pen to paper. In theory, putting pen to paper is easy. The difficult part is ensuring your message is clear regardless of the audience. And, thank you to my friends who read the content and provided great feedback. A special thank you to my son, Michael A. Hillman II 'Honey Bunny' who pushed me to get it done, as he became the first author of the family.

One Step At A Time

My wonderful husband, Dwayne, who always believed I could get it done, as I tackled work and life.

I would like to thank everyone who took the time to encourage me to take my quirky, not new thoughts and pull them together for everyone who has a desire to continue to move forward, 'one step at a time'. I offer words of encouragement, enlightenment, hope, and empowerment as you go through personal and professional triumphs.

Remembering, that life happens every day whether we like it or think we cannot handle it. I hope you can find the strength and motivation to take 'one step at a time'. So, let's get up and get moving.

One Step At A Time

One Step At A Time

One Step At A Time

Chapters

One Step At A Time

One Step At A Time

F.E.A.R.

Face Everything and Rise

Fear, is it real or imagined? Let's take a look. Have you ever fallen off a bike or skateboard? Yes, I am dating myself here, so keep up and follow along. If you have ever fallen, did you stay there, sitting on the ground or in the street? No, you got up. Maybe a little bruised, but you got up to try it again. You may have fallen multiple times, yet you continued to try to master the task. After many tries, you finally mastered the task at hand and felt pretty good about yourself. You may even tell a story about how you received the visible and almost invisible scars or said to others, never let falling keep you down.

For those of you who never got back on the bike, skateboard or the thing that made you fall, you are probably still struggling with, I cannot do this or that.

1

One Step At A Time

The 'I can't', way of thinking is a direct result of you allowing the one thing that caused you pain as a child to take over your mind as an adult. It is the same fear, just magnified because now you are worried about what others may say. I will say to you, who cares? How many times have you heard the naysayer express the following? "Wow, you did it. Or, oh my, I could never have done that." To include, "I wish I could have achieved that." They, the naysayers, have the same fear and would rather talk about how you should not try to accomplish the task at hand, rather than offer you words of encouragement to go and try it again. Those that support you will say, great job, a little effort goes a long way. I knew you could do it, or I am so excited for you, you did it. Make the decision to be in the encouraging type of company a little longer to rid your mind of the other group designed to rob you of your happiness, steal your joy, and kill your inner spirit. Trust me, you will begin to sleep a lot better, walk a bit more upright, and see yourself smiling more.

One Step At A Time

People will always have something to say - sometimes words of encouragement and other times, their own fear expressed so loudly it cannot be ignored. Those that offer you support will admire you for your ability to get past the 'thing' you struggle with and continue to encourage you. By achieving your desired goals and dreams, the naysayers that tried to stifle you by injecting their fear into your thoughts now see that you are resilient because you overcame something so difficult in their mind. The naysayer will inject their fear onto your progress because they believe they cannot do what they want to do. You must face your fears to move past the paralysis and come to the realization that you can achieve the thing that frightens you the most. Once you take the initial step forward to face your fear, the following steps become easier to navigate, one step at a time.

Now that you are thinking about what has been said, let's answer the first question posed. Is fear real or imagined? The answer, fear is real, period.

One Step At A Time

We will spend some time providing a path to get past it, so hang on.

Fear is a feeling induced by perceived danger or threat that occurs and causes a change in behavior which causes you to hide or freeze[1]. Fear is also defined as "a distressing emotion aroused by impending danger, evil, or pain whether the threat is real or imagined[2]". Fear is a negative emotion caused by a real or perceived threat to your well-being. Fear brings anxiety and worry about something we cannot control. As many medical professionals have affirmed, unchecked worry or stress can have ill-effects on our health by way of high blood pressure, obesity, headaches, heart problems, diabetes, skin conditions, asthma, arthritis, depression, and anxiety[3]. Wow! That is a lot that could go wrong with you from a physical, psychological, and mental place, all because you are afraid.

If we look at the purpose of fear, we will conclude that the emotion is there to motivate action, often avoidance and/or preparation to do something, to act. Fear is programmed into our nervous system and works like instinct.

4

One Step At A Time

We are equipped with survival instincts necessary to respond with fear when we sense danger or feel unsafe. Fear helps protect us and makes us alert to danger and prepares us to deal with the situation at hand. In the days of evolution, fear was a tool that helped us survive as we entered most situations cautiously. Key word, entered, you must enter the situation cautiously to gain the knowledge that you can and did survive whatever the incident.

Cautious and deliberate action on your part is the key to getting past what has stopped you in mid-step.

Religious scholars will cite the Bible and say that God commands us not to fear or worry, "do not fear, for I have redeemed you; I have called you by name; you are Mine"[4]. The Bible further says, 'do not be anxious about anything but in everything and in prayer and thanksgiving, present your request to God"[5]. Another perspective from the Quran says, "those who believe, and do deeds of righteousness, and establish regular prayers and regular charity, will have their reward with their Lord: on them shall be no fear, nor shall they grieve [6].

The messages in the Bible and the Quran tell us that fear is real, and you can have victory over it. So why don't we have the victory? In most cases, we have others to include ourselves in our head screaming, 'you cannot do this thing, and you should be very afraid'. Again, I will ask, why? Are you afraid because you have watched scary movies and think art will imitate life or vice versa?

Are you afraid because you had your feelings hurt and now you are protective of them? Is your fear driven by what you have always been told by the people you admire and respect that you cannot or should not? Or were you told to be grateful for what you have and where you are in life's journey and just gave up? If any of the above hold true, then you will never move forward or accomplish your goals. There will always be the little voice of other people deciding what is best for you.

One Step At A Time

Only you can make the decision to confront your fears and celebrate when you reach the other side. If the lesson of the action is an oops moment, then guess what, you will not do that again and thus, been an apt pupil and received the lesson and experience.

If the lesson is an achievement, then guess what, you will have reached the desired end state of an accomplishment.

When we replace fear with curiosity, it opens us up and brings in enthusiasm. The thoughts of fear are replaced with the thoughts of inquisitiveness. Therefore, be more curious. Replace the negative thoughts of, 'I am afraid they will not like my idea' with; 'I am curious to know how this will actually turn out'. Work to become an interested person who is open to new ideas and experiences. Put your fearful thoughts in perspective by asking the following questions:

What is the worst that can happen if my fears come true?

What is the best outcome possible for me if I act, despite my fear?

One Step At A Time

Once you know the answers or have accomplished the task at hand, you can take the next step as long as there is no danger to yourself or others. Remember to be intentional with whatever the decision is, trust your positive instincts, and turn away from the fearful thoughts.

"Do not be the thermometer that is driven and dictated by your surroundings."

Be the thermostat that dictates the environment.

Author Unknown

8

The Power of Resilience

I hope you find the strength and motivation to take one step at a time and become resilient, recovering quickly. Why one step and why resilient? What other options do you have? It is easy to just stop and wait out fear, or is it? You must ask yourself, what am I waiting for? What am I afraid of? Most will say, of failing. I would say, that is how we learn; failure is proof we are trying and that is called experience. There are really no absolutes in life other than tomorrow will come and as the sun rises, we get another opportunity to try it all over again. Like the bike analogy, you must get up and keep moving to overcome the anxiety of falling.

Why resilient? Because you can recover. You can snap back into action and keep moving. The objective is to learn from the situation and then move forward. You must first try before you have failed and then, try it again. Remember the bike and skateboard attempts? I know, I keep referring to riding that dreadful contraption. Guess what?

One Step At A Time

That dreadful contraption is the key to your initial interaction with overcoming your fear. And, if you are honest with yourself, you probably still tell stories about how you overcame this obstacle when you see a child starting to learn how to ride a bicycle. Therefore, you might fall however, you can get up and keep trying until the skill is mastered. If what you are trying to achieve were easy, then everyone would have achieved the same goal.

If we do not try there is no growth and development. Continuous learning will yield a better version of yourself, so keep your mind active, which keeps you relevant.

Ponder this: if no one took the necessary steps to ask, "what if", we would still be listening to the radio for our news or sitting in front of a black and white television without Technicolor. Our music would not have evolved past vinyl/wax albums, 8-track, cassette tapes, MP3, CD, and the option to stream music would not exist.

Where we are today with the advancements of technology and streaming is because someone kept trying.

One Step At A Time

Our clothing would not have the great vibrant colors and different fabrics, the only car color would be black and the thought of automatic, hybrid or electric versions of the automobile would not exist. There are medical marvels that exist because of failure and the continuous attempts to try again. We applaud those that said, let's try one more time, as they drive our effort of continuous curiosity, growth, and learning, so thank you!

Let's think back to a time when you either smiled or laughed out loud. You know when something was genuinely funny. Let's think of three good things that happened to you today. I am sure you can find three, no matter how simple, just good things. Use the space below to capture those thoughts for reflection when you feel overwhelmed. The note will allow you to return to a place that offers peace and tranquility, and who knows, you might smile or laugh out loud again, releasing the stress and thoughts of you cannot.

One Step At A Time

1.

2.

3.

"The future is made by those who create it."

Author Unknown

12

Staying True to Yourself

Staying true to yourself. What does that mean, why does it matter, and who cares? Staying true to yourself provides insight into your moral compass. Okay, so wait a minute, before you get ahead of yourself let's discuss you and what makes you the person you are. Are you pretending at work? Pretending to be a good person? Pretending to know your job? Eventually you will receive questions from your peers and maybe your supervisor. You will be expected to know the answer or where to locate the answer. If you are obtaining the answer from a peer and pass it along as your truth, there may be an integrity issue at hand. Or at worst case, a lack of morals. If you do not know the answer own it and when you find the answer, give credit to the person that assisted you in obtaining the answer. This small act says you are a team player, an honest person, someone that will do the right thing when others are looking and when they are not. As a side note, you will not get away with being a fraud, eventually the truth will reveal itself therefore, when you act, you must know the consequences of your actions.

13

One Step At A Time

Yes, 'to thine own self be true, and if you are true to yourself, then it naturally follows that you will be true to others too"[7]. So, what is meant by, know the consequences of your actions and why offer, to thine own self be true? The cause and effect, if you do this or that, then this or that will occur. If you are ok with knowing the cause and effect, then go forth and congratulations on conquering your fear(s).

If you do not know the consequences or are not good with the possible outcomes, then do not attempt the task. You must know what will happen if you do the thing at hand. Yes, you might fail, consequence.

Then you try again and do not attempt the thing that caused you to fail again, effect. What is the old saying, how do you know unless you try? Or nothing beats a failure (because he did not try) but a try (because he might succeed).

Why does staying true to yourself matter, and why should you care? This is your life, and you must first be comfortable in it.

14

One Step At A Time

Only you can decide what is best for you. Yes, your family and close friends might have gotten to a place where you want to be. They are debt-free, have traveled the world, saved money, and reached the top of their professional career ladder. Let those you admire become your benchmark, the motivation you can use to go your own way and focus on your goals. Try hard to ignore the naysayers. They want to drain your dreams and inject fear into your life.

The William Shakespeare quote, 'to thine own self'… is relevant as you do not want to do or say anything that would cause your word to be worthless. All we have is our word and our brand which reflects you, your center, your core, your substance of existence.

Once your word, core, or substance is nullified, what is left? Own the fear or mistake and take ownership of the actions and/or pain you have caused.

Offer an apology, even if time has passed and you think the offended person has forgotten what you may have said or did to them.

One Step At A Time

Our actions may have been a flippant comment, unsupported and unsolicited advice. Go and make it right.

Maybe your actions were a knee-jerk reaction to prevent others from seeing your fear or being revealed as a fraud. A fraud in the sense of being afraid of something, the initial fear that is driving your actions. Is it the bike or something else? Only you know the answer. You do not want anyone to know that you gave up and failed at the task at hand. Thus, you sit in silence and treat others poorly. We do this, because deep down, we never owned the lack of doing the deed that haunts us in our minds. Our childhood never escapes us, and thus, we must own it and move on. Always tell the truth and be trustworthy with the smallest of things.

So here is the quandary, the fear, the hesitation, the real issue. The fear of failing, the thought of failing. Whatever you want to call it. The thing that stops you in your tracks. The thing that keeps you up at night, caught in your own daydream.

One Step At A Time

If you take one step at a time, you will come through whatever is holding you back, this is for certain.

Now, think of it this way. What would happen (cause) if you did whatever it is (effect)? Can you see it? Then go get it. You must take the first step to be successful. Think of your days in a classroom. Every class starts with an 'A'. Your final grade will depend on how much effort, or the lack thereof, revealing the consequences of the effort given - positive or negative. If you run the stop light or exceed the speed limit (cause) your actions may result in a ticket (effect).

We can make split decisions about most things in life, except areas that are unfamiliar to us. Here is the thing, you blindly trust the global positioning system (GPS) as it instructs you to turn right or left, taking you to a place that you are unfamiliar, hence the use of the application. Then it happens, you turn right or left (cause) onto a road that leads to a place you were not trying to go (effect). You panic, the GPS says, 'redirecting' and then you start over still trying to reach your destination.

One Step At A Time

When you finally arrive, you are relieved and moving on to the task at hand. The next time the GPS tells you to turn down the same street to a place you did not want to go. You may think and say out loud, I already know that is not the correct way to go and you go the other way and save time and frustration.

The cause and effect of knowing the consequences of your actions is profound when placed in perspective.

Let's take the interview you did not prepare for. You used a resume you did not write, check, or was not an honest representation of your skills. It was embellished to show you as the best candidate. What does the adage say? "Success is where preparation and opportunity intersect"[8]. First, is it okay to have someone else write your resume based on 'your input'? Yes. You may not know how to paint a clear picture of your skills.

You may also not know how to measure your accomplishments. Or, to show a clear picture of your skills. A little help is always a good thing. Also, the skills should be yours, not someone else's.

One Step At A Time

You should be able to speak to them. Do not present yourself to a team of people during the interview who have knowledge of the job and skills required to do said job. Let me share a brief story.

We were interviewing this person, let's call him Jack, for a training position. I asked Jack how he felt about the ADDIE model.

Jack's response was, "I do not know 'her', but I may have heard about 'her'". I was stunned at his response, and I believe everyone in the room was also. In the training world, ADDIE (Analyze, Design, Develop, Implement, and Evaluate) is the cornerstone of training.

I say okay, let me give Jack the benefit of the doubt. Maybe he is just nervous as his resume reads that he is a training guru. I ask a follow-on question. What methods of assessment do you prefer when evaluating training? Jack's response, "just ask if they liked it". He did not mention the Kirkpatrick or the Phillips ROI desired models.

I was done, and so was Jack from further consideration. Guess what? Jack's resume got him in the room; yet Jack never made it past the table. You should be able to speak to what is on the paper, to include your knowledge, skills, and abilities with passion.

The industry expects you to know the language and the actions it will take to be successful in the position. Do you know the industry acronyms and steps to reach or do the task for which you are seeking employment? Check what is said about you in your resume and be able to speak to it when asked with many examples.

You may already be aware of the below 'tips' yet, let's do a refresher for some common oops moments:

1. Do your research on the organization/company you are seeking employment. They might ask you what you know about their business.

2. Never lie/embellish on your resume; again, they might ask you about that one line.

3. Arrive early. If you are on time, you are already late.

One Step At A Time

4. Dress for the position you are seeking. There are some caveats to this one. If you are applying for a warehouse position, then arriving in a tuxedo is not the best option for the interview.

5. If you are applying for an office position, your after-five club attire is not the best option for the interview. This is a future workplace, even in a virtual environment, not the after-party.

6. Remove your chewing gum. Turn off your cell phone during this time.

7. Bring copies of your resume in case you need to refer to it.

8. Have pen and paper to take notes.

9. When the question has two parts, note the first part to avoid forgetting the initial question and not providing a full response.

10. Smile and try to relax.

One Step At A Time

The ten items above are a few examples of what might occur. Remember, we are still staying true to ourselves in all things. Think of this: those on the interview panel do not know you. What you wrote represents you and your brand therefore, have an idea of what is on the paper.

You must be able to say why you are the best person for the job and a good fit in the organization. The panel is interviewing you and you should be interviewing them as well. Why are you interviewing them you ask? Because the environment or those interviewing you may be goofy and you realize this is not the environment you want to be a part of. They may be unprofessional discussing office personal business in your presence, using vulgar words, and just not nice people. If this is the best the company has to offer to recruit its talent, beware and use this interview as practice for the next one.

Expect questions like, tell us about yourself. What are your hobbies? What would your last supervisor have to say about you, note, last, not current. Provide 3-5 adjectives that would describe you.

One Step At A Time

Tell us about your greatest failure and how you overcame the objective? What is your greatest accomplishment to date? And the proverbial, why should we hire you over the other candidates? Okay that was more than a few; how many could you answer without stumbling?

Do your homework and arrive prepared. In most cases, you get the interview because you meet the initial qualifications. Now it is time to sell your skills and your bubbling personality to get the job.

Do not change who you are to fit into someone else's mold. At the end of the day, you will not like or respect the person looking back at you in the mirror. Do not alter your values or beliefs for 'likes'.

At the end of the day, you will not like or respect the person looking back at you in the mirror.

And finally, take care of yourself first; an empty cup cannot fill another cup. What is the goal, to like yourself first and be a person of integrity.

One Step At A Time

"If we never try, we shall never succeed."

Abraham Lincoln

24

One Step At A Time

Taking Deliberate Steps Forward

Now we have identified what causes us to fear the unknown. We have also discovered how to remain resilient and stay true to ourselves. So, let's take some deliberate life steps. Some of you reading this book may say, I already know this and that is great. Will you share what you have learned with others? For those that may be a little foggy on the subject here we go.

Basic savings…

If your goal is to save money, then you may need to take some deliberate steps to reach this goal. Consider stop eating out as much, this includes ordering from the places that deliver your food. Pack a lunch from dinner leftovers. It is okay to splurge once a week as this will keep you motivated to save. If you drink expensive coffee, can you make your own with their brand and take it with you? The price per bag is cheaper than the 'venti or extra-large' you order daily. Have you done the basic math on your purchases?

One Step At A Time

Do you know how much you have spent on food and drinks purchased in the last week or month?

Purchasing items that are not on sale is never a good idea. Paying full price is not advisable when the item will go on sale by the next holiday or season change. I am sure you have clothing in your closet that is a season or two behind that you still wear. I am also sure you have heard this all before and are knowledgeable on how to penny pinch, so let's move on to some other areas to consider.

The intent is to provide food for thought. Can you take a little from each paycheck and place the funds into a high-yield savings account? If your company has a 401k plan that offers matching, are you contributing enough to get the matching? Did I mention, that by saving pre-tax you will be taxed on less and your check may not be much less, and you have saved a little bit more for your retirement. By not making the required contribution, you leave the 'free' money on the table, and this is not advisable. Some will say to have a long-term and a short-term savings. Long-term savings is for big things.

One Step At A Time

A long-term savings may include a wedding, honeymoon, car or home purchase, vacation, and furniture. This savings also includes a non-employer-based 401K plan for retirement. Long-term savings helps you save and pay off debt. The action allows you to create lasting memories without the extra cost.

The short-term fund is for emergencies and covers six months of your living expenses. The expenses may include your rent/mortgage, electric, gas, cell phone bill, car insurance, renters' insurance, cable, and internet. Think of the six months as security because you never know what will happen. An example could be for a tire purchase because you will get a flat. If you have an accident, do you have your deductible? When the insurance company writes the check, the deductible will be subtracted from the insurance check. Also, consider an outfit, shoes, purse, or belt you were eyeing. You can make the purchase because you have saved for it. You will look up and your small contributions per pay day will turn into three digits, then one comma and then maybe two commas.

One Step At A Time

The objective is everyone can save something by making the conscience effort to deny one small thing that will become a greater thing in time.

If you give yourself an allowance and save from it, you can make the fun purchase without debt. Notice that credit cards are not mentioned. If you have them, focus on getting rid of them. Paying the minimum amount due, plus the interest will lower the balance. Then, round up to the nearest dollar and stop using the card.

Pay the cards with the highest interest first, as you are paying more to rent the charge. Wait, do you know the interest rate of your credit card(s)? Do you know how much it costs to use the credit cards when you swipe? If not, that is your homework. If so, let's focus on getting rid of them.

One Step At A Time

A place to live ...

To buy your first home, money is required. Remember, we are still talking about deliberate steps forward. There are fees involved and here are a few: closing costs, which you may or may not have help. The buyer must pay for the appraisal to verify the home's value. You must also pay for a home inspection. The inspection ensures the major components are in good working order.

These components are the heating, ventilation, air conditioning, electrical, roofing, plumbing, and there is not an issue with the foundation. You must also pay for the first year of homeowner's insurance. Say you do not want to buy a traditional home. You would rather have a tiny house that fits you. The same fees and other costs may apply.

You may want a condo by the lake or overlooking the mountains. What are the monthly assessments and what do they cover? Sometimes the assessments are as much as the monthly mortgage.

One Step At A Time

You may have even considered trying to take part in the 'van life' to save money. Great, now let's factor in where you will bathe? Gym memberships, truck stops, and/or golf/boating clubs are options. How will you eat, cook in, or eat out? Where will you park? Open parking lots, campgrounds, or stealthy in a neighborhood? Or will you say forget it and try to find a roommate or remain at your parents' home and save your money if that is an option.

University versus Junior College …

We are already aware that the cost of college is as much as a home purchase in some places and the cost is increasing yearly. For those with young kids they will grow up and look to you to pay for them to attend college. Wait, does the teenager know that college is not an extension of high school and there is a cost associated with attending? If you are a homeowner, then your property tax covers the cost of high school. Now we are talking about an additional cost to cover college. Are you kids aware that college is not free?

One Step At A Time

Looks like it is time to have the college conversation maybe at the middle school level to help the young person understand the value in achieving good grades and volunteering.

Let's discuss the purpose of a college degree, certifications, and trade schools. Some professions need a college degree and experience in the field.

The degree shows the employer that you can think and complete long-term projects. You can work over the summers in the field of your degree while a student to obtain some experiences. Working in the field builds your resume and provides experience. You can cut the cost of the four-year degree by attending the local junior college to get the general education courses for less. Then, transfer to the university to finish the last two years. If your field requires a college degree and you lack one, you will be at a disadvantage in the job attainment process.

Now, if you are the person seeking to attend college do not act on the emotion of, my friends are going to college, and I want to join them.

31

One Step At A Time

Do you know how they are paying for college? If not, visit the junior college to get the same basic courses for less. Do not create a bill and then return home after the first semester or year in debt. Do the math and consider the best option to prevent incurring a bill that you could have reduced or even avoided.

Consider the junior college that teaches skilled and certified trades. There will always be a need for the plumber, roofer, and electrician. Do not forget about the heating, ventilation, and cooling experts, solar installers, carpenters, and welders.

Without the skilled trades, we would not have buildings or paved roads. We would not have homes, nurses, and other medical fields. We also would not have the safe environments we take for granted. The skilled trades are the bedrock of our society. They may not wear a suit and tie or have glamours titles however, they hold the world, yes world, together.

One Step At A Time

If one of the trades gets you excited, take some time to visit that skill in its environment to obtain a real look into how it works and ask questions. The trades are needed every day and in every country. When you need something fixed or built, you call a skilled tradesperson. Is that you answering the call?

The fairy tale wedding...

The wedding that does not pay for itself. What do I mean you ask? All weddings should cover their own expenses. The gifts that are given to cover the cost of the meal meet the bare minimum standard. Most people are not aware their gift should cover the cost of their meal. Now you can spend over $40,000 on your wedding. This cost may cover the rings, venue, meal, and cake. It may also cover the dress, shoes, and tuxedo. Do not forget about the invitations, photographer, limousines, music, decorations, and parting gifts. And that's just a few examples.

Or, you could have a smaller ceremony with the justice of the peace or clergy. Then, go to dinner with those you see every day to celebrate the occasion.

You can always have the party to acknowledge the event, or not. Who is the big event for, other people or you and your loved one? What is the intent of the fairy tale? That same $40,000 is a nice downpayment on a place to live, can be applied to your student loans, or a vacation of a lifetime. Once you have paid off your debt, you can also use the money to create lasting memories.

I am not saying you should skip the fairy tale wedding if you saved for it. Do not go into debt to have it. The amount of debt you carry, including student loans, and weddings, reduces your purchasing power of obtaining the bricks and sticks of a residence, if that is your goal.

Are you still thinking about your next steps? Great! The three items mentioned are a sampling of where your money finds a home. Oh, did we discuss the expense of having children?

One Step At A Time

To stay home or not to stay home after the birth? Wait, you must go to work because your debt (student loan, mortgage, wedding, and so on) requires it. Remember other expenses like daycare, diapers, formula, and clothing come with children.

Your bundle of joy will outgrow clothes and diapers so fast, and we have not discussed the cost of milk. Oh, did you say you will nurse?

That is wonderful, you must eat and drink more to have milk production for the child to receive. Whew, that is a lot and the cost keep adding up.

Have you given any consideration to your thoughts and how they may affect your ability to move forward? Do you have a plan to get to the end of the desired path? Do you have a better understanding of where you are? Do you feel better as you are progressing towards your goals and dreams? These are a few questions to make you go hum… as you take deliberate steps to move forward.

One Step At A Time

The dream job…

What is the dream job or career? Are you chasing money or passion, as they both matter. If you are chasing the passion to do what you love, then you already have your 'dream job/career'. To have peace means you are in a profession where, if you would do what you are currently doing and were not paid you would continue to come to work.

The compensation for your knowledge and skills is the gravy on top. The ice cream with your pie and the sprinkles on top of the treat. Work should not be a chore. Yet, you must first have an idea about what it is that excites you and makes you get up on Monday morning to do it.

If you are chasing money, then you will not have peace. You will always have your ear to the ground. Your laptop will be open to the classifieds. You will also be networking with your friends for the next raise. Do not get what I am saying wrong. Money pays for a place to live and all that comes with it.

36

One Step At A Time

Money affords you the ability to visit the places on your bucket list. Money also is the means to remove your monthly debt (credit cards and car loans), so you do need it. Yet, let's stay focused on the dream job/career, what that looks like, and why. I will offer, to never chase money.

Do the best that you can every day, and the money will come. If you think, I am interviewing for my next position each day that I show up to work, amazing things will happen. You will be noticed, and informed when advancement opportunities are available. Someone will say to you – hey, I saw this position and thought of you. Or, hey, so and so is looking for someone to… and I gave them your name. When interviewing, your professional self is on display. The interview panel will see your value as you speak the language of the position and provide great examples of your accomplishments when asked. You never know who is watching so, do what is good and what is right, because it is the right thing to do.

One Step At A Time

Entrepreneurship...

The American way is through capitalism. Ownership and opportunity are key components of capitalism, which add supply and demand. As a business owner, you must be able to identify the demand and provide the goods and services to meet that demand.

You may not want to work for anyone. You want to be the one who provides jobs by offering your product. Entrepreneurship has many benefits that include, financial and creative independence, and a better work-life balance to name a few. Through your business, you will be able to develop new markets. You will help the economy grow. You will have a positive impact on others and your customers. You will network with other business owners and make more money.

The Small Business Administration says small businesses are the backbone of the United States (U.S.) economy. Small businesses account for 44% of the U.S. economic activity and 99.9% of the American job market.

One Step At A Time

Chase your dreams of entrepreneurship and align your business with what gets you jazzed. Remember, the creation of your small business must fill a need that is in demand to generate the wealth you seek.

Remember, having more money will not address your financial concerns. You must first manage the one dollar you have before you can manage the ten you may receive. Second, you must understand what you want. Then, you must take deliberate steps towards your goals.

Your health...

Improving your physical and mental health can lead to longer more productive years as you continue to thrive. Why is this important? Studies from Harvard Health, National Library of Medicine, and Johns Hopkins University to name a few, have shown that regular exercise, rest, and a good diet can boost self-esteem, mood, sleep quality, energy level, and reduces stress.

One Step At A Time

You can help increase your heart and blood flow by running, walking, cycling, playing tennis, pickle ball, swimming or any activity that gets your heart rate up for 30 minutes at least five days a week. Regular exercise can do remarkable things to your mind, body and spirit. Of course, consult with your doctor before you begin any exercise routine.

If you cannot go outside, there are exercises online you can do at home that yield great benefits. Try chair and wall exercises and use your own body weight to tone and define your muscles. If you can go out, start by walking to the corner, then to the next block, and have a goal to double your routine every week. Walking is less jarring to the body and if you can take a brisk walk, talk or sing along the way, you are doing great.

Please do not think exercise is only for a younger person. Exercise is good for everyone due to the many health benefits that come by way of just moving. When you factor in a healthy diet that consist of green leafy vegetable, fruits, whole grains, lean protein, plenty of water, and portion control. You should be able to see your plate once your food groups have been added.

Why are we discussing your health, because your health plays an important role in your mood, behavior and helps you to thrive at every turn. If you can, take a daily break and walk to the mailbox, end of the driveway, or to the corner, smell the air, listen to nature, and watch the animals play. You will find that your stress has been reduced and you are able to stay engaged mentally. Remember, we are taking deliberate steps forward and a healthy lifestyle is a part of those steps. Let's turn off the cell phone, laptop, and television to get a good night rest so that we can face the next day ready, willing, and able.

One Step At A Time

"The best way to predict the future is to create it."

Abraham Lincoln

Always Speak Your Truth

Can you speak your truth with respect and compassion? Can you do so without losing yourself or insulting others?

First let's ensure we are on the same page as we define respect and compassion. The Oxford dictionary defines respect as "deep admiration for someone's feelings, wishes, or rights." Compassion is sympathetic concern for the sufferings or misfortunes of others. To speak your truth, you must do so from a place of genuine care. Not trying to convince, compel, or control the conversation, situation, or person. To use harsh words to express yourself is rude. To belittle others to express yourself is also rude and insulting.

How did you get your way as a child and are you displaying those same mannerisms as an adult? Only you know the truth. I bet you are behaving the same way, and no one told you that your behavior was unacceptable. Here we are many years later, yielding the same outcome. Remember, we are not trying to force or control.

43

One Step At A Time

We are also not trying to persuade anyone or any situation. I am sure you have heard people say, 'that is how they are'. Does this mean the world has to succumb to Jack's antics? No, we do not. Jack must learn to play well with others. We live in a civilized society where people are polite towards one another. If we are not civilized towards one another, there will be anarchy and unrest everywhere. You can speak your truth with respect and compassion and as you do, not offend others. You can play nice.

We must approach our conversation with civility and an open heart. In doing so, your words will come across a little softer. Now, do not misunderstand what is being said. You can stand firm in your position as long as you allow others to remain firm in their position. You listen to understand and not to inject the first opportunity there is a pregnant pause.

One Step At A Time

You listen from a place of understanding. Not to prepare your response while the other person is speaking. Conversations two-way that requires one to actively listen and then speak. Ask clarifying questions to ensure you understand before you respond.

Speak with the intent to communicate your needs. Share your ideas with compassion, using your inside voice to ensure you are heard. The moment someone feels disrespected or not heard, they will shut down and the conversation is over. Remember to enter the conversation with compassion. Your thoughts and the thoughts of others demand respect and it is okay to disagree.

"I have learned that people will forget what you said, forget what you did but people will never forget how you made them feel."

Maya Angelou

45

One Step At A Time

Happiness Defined

You define your happiness; not what others tell you what happiness should resemble. What a thought, I get to say what makes me happy, mic drop! Parents have advised high school graduates to attend college or learn a skilled trade. If neither of those interests you, visit Uncle Sam by way of the military. Your military service will fill the gap while you figure out your life. Some would also say you need a job with benefits and a pension. A job with benefits because you hope to reach 60 years old (or whatever retirement age is), are eligible to retire, and can. Are these options still true today? Let's take a deep dive.

Going to college is an option if the person has an idea about what they want to do in life. Most do not at 17 or 18. Now, some have taken jobs to dabble in an interesting field. Others have worked in areas they know they want nothing to do with as an adult. So, some have a slight idea. If a person lacks the resources to attend an institution of higher learning post high school, they should attend a junior college.

One Step At A Time

At the junior college they can take the basic education requirements, English, math, and history. Every student must complete the general education courses, and they cost less at the junior college. That is, unless someone else is paying their education bill through scholarship. Otherwise, the student will be home after the first semester and with a bill in hand. The same money would have gone a lot further at the junior college, just saying. You prefer hands-on learning over classroom instruction. A trade school offers a great way to earn a living while acquiring a lifelong skill.

There will always be a need for skilled nurses and the other medical trade technicians. You know them as the phlebotomist, x-ray technician, radiology technician, ultra-sound technician, pharmacy technician, medical and dental assistants. Now let's add the electricians, plumbers, roofers, carpenters, solar installers, cosmetologists, and nail technicians because beauty has a cost, to the list.

One Step At A Time

The military option is always there when none of the other options will work. The military will provide a trade through education.

They will also provide three meals a day, a place to sleep, medical insurance, physical training, and benefits after four years of training. The earned benefits will be useful during and after exiting the service for a lifetime. Not to mention, the travel and a cash down payment on a home is not required.

Other benefits include, the ability to get a small business loan as a Veteran, money for college after the fact through the GI Bill, and free college through tuition assistance, while on active duty. Oh, did I mention you will get paid on the 1st and 15th of the month for the skills you learn in school that you will do every day. There is also a pension you will receive when you are retirement age.

The military offers the best plan when there is not one to fill the growth gap. Some will say take the 'gap year'. I will say at what cost? Delaying taking responsibility for yourself as an adult is not the answer. It is delaying the inevitable.

One Step At A Time

Taking the time to think about what excites you and taking the steps to chase that excitement is growth. If you are standing still, you are not growing. If you are standing still, who is incurring the cost while you stand? If we are not encouraging our kids and young adults to chase what excites them early, then plan to foot the 'gap year' bill later.

So, as you say to your kids, nieces, and nephews, what do you want to do after high school? Let's begin to have a different conversation in middle school. Let's try what do you like to do? What brings a smile to your face?

You too may learn something from the fifth grader. They have no walls or self-imposed limits. You can also ask yourself the same questions. What brings you joy? What gets you jazzed? What would you like to do if you were not paid one cent? Ah ha! Now you are thinking. That is the thing to pursue.

If you are not in middle or high school, graduated college, or earned a trade certificate, how do you define happiness? It depends on your definition and what you are looking for in life. Ask yourself, what gets me jazzed? What would I do if I were not paid to do it?

I know we asked this of the middle schoolers earlier, as stated, the same questions can apply to you too.

What are your options? Let's look at a few we have covered now that you are thinking. Would you like a better job? Better in the sense it has benefits and an increase in your pay. Well, we discussed that option, seek and you will find.

Do you want to get married or find a healthy sustaining relationship? You must get out there and meet people. Remember, every interaction with someone is not a proposal to marriage. It is an interaction/date to get to know them better. Leave your list at home and just have fun.

You desire a better relationship with others, first - you must be a friend to get a friend. You want to have more money left in your checking account after you have paid the basic living expenses. We discussed the deliberate steps to savings.

51

One Step At A Time

We have learned so much from the global pandemic about what is important, and our focus has shifted. Do what gets you jazzed and puts a smile on your face. This may take a while as you work out the debt thing, which we already discussed.

However, you must have a plan to be able to take one step. Work to place yourself in a position where you can make a move to something more rewarding and not just log on or show up to a place for the check. Look down the road and focus on reaching what will bring your full potential to life.

People will always place their limitations on you because they already believe they cannot so you cannot either. Their fear will become your fear, and you will not realize when it happened, as the conversation is so subtle. Oh man, you cannot do that. What if you fail, what if they laugh at you? What if it does not work? What if…

All because they are afraid of change and the unknown. Remember, change is good, it is how we grow. There is nothing you cannot do.

One Step At A Time

Unless you have tried to do it and failed at it, tried again, and again, so, go and try before you say you cannot. And then, try again.

The spark of genius is just another try away and remember, whatever you desire, it all begins with one step at a time.

"The pessimist sees difficulty in every opportunity. The optimist sees opportunity in every difficulty."

Winston Churchill

One Step At A Time

One Step At A Time

The Rearview Mirror

For those of us who drive or have been a passenger in a car, you are familiar with the rear-view mirror and its purpose. The rearview mirror lets us see behind the car. We use it as we try to change lanes and move forward.

Life is like driving a car. We get in, set a destination in mind, and then traverse the road to get there. In life, we get up and groom ourselves. Then, we grab a cup of your favorite drink and hit the road to a set destination.

Here is the thought. Have you ever tried to walk to a place backward? Walking backward the entire time would be impossible. You cannot arrive to a destination that requires driving by walking backward. Well, you could, it would take a while longer. The same is true in driving. You will not reach your destination traveling in reverse.

One Step At A Time

What will take place is an accident as you can only focus on the direction of forward travel. There is no way we can get to a destination safely in reverse.

Let's stop looking in the rearview mirror as we seek to travel forward in life. Okay, so how is this accomplished? By not focusing on what happened behind you. You cannot change the action therefore, let's take the path of not making the same mistake again. You know the definition of insanity? Doing the same thing over and over and expecting a different result[9]. This is truly not the goal here, as we are not insane. To move forward in any action, we must be all in. We cannot focus on the past. We learn from past actions and make different decisions next time. The lesson in taking a different path is knowing progress is not always forward. Sometimes progress must move left or right to go forward and gain your footing.

Now that we know the purpose of the rearview mirror. Let's use it as intended, to check for past actions and ensure that our left and right are safe to proceed. Yes, left and right would be the side mirrors in action also.

We have assumed it is safe to move forward, so why don't we? That dang fear thing again. The fear of, it might not work out. What if it does work out and is the best decision you have made? You will not know the result unless you stop looking behind you and focus on what is ahead of you.

Life has so much to offer. When we open our mind, we see the wide-eyed, ecstatic, sun-driven world. We see flowers blooming, hear streams running, and gaze at the snowcapped mountains ahead. We must put one foot in front of the other. Take the necessary steps to do the task at hand, accomplishing life, and life, more abundantly.

"Continuous improvement is better than delayed perfection."

Mark Twain

One Step At A Time

58

No Finish-line

Not stopping and moving the goal line to provide continual growth. Always asking, what's next? Think about it. If we stop moving, what may happen? Nothing. Exactly! We must think of our lives as a living testimony. What is next after we meet a goal? Movement keeps our minds active and prevents disease and stagnation. Think of nature. Each new season allows living things bloom. That living blossoming thing can provide what others need to thrive. We should take care of our lives to do the same, cross-pollinating what is in you to what you project outwardly. Giving back at every opportunity, offering other living organisms the ability to continue to grow.

What do you know you can achieve and maybe receive the reward or acknowledgement later? Are you able and willing to put the work in to make that goal a reality?

One Step At A Time

Life is not a contradiction. You can be nervous and excited about the unknown. Two emotions can exist at once, this is known as mixed emotions, and it is a common human experience to feel a blend of emotions in any given situation. It is ok to have some anxiety, just do not stop moving.

There are no hard stops or absolutes in life. Life is what we choose it to be. Remember, the conversation about fear? Your hope for a better tomorrow or a tomorrow that is enough - is possible because you kept moving. Hope must be greater than fear to move you forward. Do not stay in the negative emotions too long. Those thoughts will drain you, cause you to become immobile, a state of paralysis and make fear a reality.

We may have finished one task; yet there are so many other things you can do for yourself and for others to keep moving. It is okay to take a breath and embrace your accomplishments. Once you have achieved that hard thing, you gain momentum. You move the goalpost a little more, seeking what is next.

One Step At A Time

Live your life with trusted, verified facts. Do not live with the illusion of what you think is real. As the saying goes, trust but verify.

The only finish line is death. Did you live your best life out loud? Did you achieve the desires of your heart? If so, fantastic. If not, try again before there is a date on the other side of the dash. Yes, when there is no more you in the physical sense of the word.

What will your family and others say about you? Acknowledging, we do not live for what others may say. We live for what we desire and dream of. However, as life goes, we will leave the flesh and bones and there will be a conversation surrounding the life you lived. Maybe they will not say what you think they will say, and the conversation will be more like, what they thought of you and all your great accomplishments. Maybe, they will say that you cared for others. You were always trying to help, and you gave unconditionally to name a few.

Notice I did not speak to the negative. There will always be someone to say something unflattering. We cannot prevent those comments.

One Step At A Time

However, we do not have to contribute to negative comments either. Continue to work on being the best version of yourself. Continue to learn and advocate for yourself first and then others.

Be intentional with your life to leave a path others can travel and learn from. You should always be in motion, always growing, and never standing, unless you are enjoying then view.

"Move forward with purpose."

Sherrilyn Kenyon

The Power of 'I Can'

Let's return to your happy place. Be it your childhood or when you were a young adult and figured out life was not hard. Life is a time in space that requires action. Life yields the consequences of your actions. These consequences provide experiences to help you make better choices. Wherever that inner happy place is for you, embrace your inner inquisitive self. Place one foot in front of the other, taking one step at a time, towards your desired goals. Go to the place before you were taught to be afraid and put action in place, one step at a time to move forward.

Do you know how we warn others or are warned to be careful to avoid falling, getting hurt, or failing? We scream, "be careful, you might fall down". Take that fear of falling, getting hurt and or failing and try the task at hand. It is not what you did that caused you to not achieve the identified task at hand. It was the action that was taken afterwards. Let's think about that.

One Step At A Time

Remember the bicycle? You must get up and try again and again and yet again. Each time we try, we learn something different. We learn what not to do and what will not work.

We can thank many people for who we are. The thanks you would extend to our family, friends, and acquaintances. Also, thanking random people we follow on social media. Each person has provided a little seed that has added value to who we are, how we think, and behave. Be mindful of those little seeds that are planted. We want to gain deep roots of experiences - positive or negative - as we learn from both to reflect upon and share.

We will need a wide stance to provide solid footing when the storm and fear arrive. The storm and fear will try to steal your bright spots so remember; the storm will pass. We will need shade to protect against the light of temporary excitement, the ruse.

The seeds symbolize the people around you and their subliminal effect on you. With that, be careful who you allow to plant in your garden.

64

One Step At A Time

You have seen how you are made, the stuff you call you. You now know for sure, what makes up your thoughts and actions. You can take the steps to make the needed changes. The change or the butterfly effect, will alter your journey to your goals as you get through each day. You know what drives you to think - and so act.

You can change the input to yield a different outcome, if you are not satisfied with the results thus far. Now that you have seen behind the curtain of your life, you can make the edits to the ingredients to change the outcome.

Sometimes, when you see yourself in real time, the reflection in the mirror can seem out of focus. Take the time to reflect on some of your decisions to bring the reflection into focus. You may think it is too late to change and become a better version of yourself. It is not too late to take your life by the horns. Act now. Move one step at a time, against life's pressure. Make small changes that reflect who you are today versus who you were yesterday. The goal is to learn from the past to have a different impact on the future.

One Step At A Time

You are not your past unless there is no action by you to make the required changes. Each season is a chance to bloom. A time to provide what is needed for yourself and others that depend upon you to flourish. Now what? Grant yourself grace and learn from your mistakes so that they are not repeated. If the same mistakes keep happening, it is safe to say you did not learn from them.

You have the power to decide your life outcomes. You have the power to drive your goals forward. You have the power to change the future, 'one step at a time.' You have the power of, I can.

"If you can't fly then run, if you can't run then walk, if you can't walk then crawl, but whatever you do you have to keep moving forward."

Martin Luther King Jr.

References

1. Dictionary.com

2. Mayo Clinic

3. Isaiah 43:1 King James Version

4. Philippians 4:4-7 King James Version

5. Qur'an Chapter 2: 277

6. William Shakespeare – Hamlet

7. Zig Ziglar

8. Albert Einstein

One Step At A Time

Notes

About the Author

Tanya R. Hellams was born in Chicago, Illinois. She now lives on the east coast with her husband, Dwayne. They have five children. Their children live in Chicago and Kankakee Illinois, Houston Texas, Jacksonville Florida, and Atlanta Georgia. They also have twelve grandchildren. Tanya is a dual-service Veteran, serving in the United States Air Force and retiring from the United States Navy with over 21 years of total service. She has over 30 years of motivating others thru her work at the Chicago Transit Authority, in military service, with the State of Illinois Department of Veterans Affairs and as a federal civil servant. She has worked at the United States Department of Veterans Affairs, United States Patent and Trademark Office, and the United States Department of Energy. In each position, Tanya provided guidance and motivation to her peers, new and seasoned supervisors, as well as newly appointed senior executives.

One Step At A Time

She has helped those that call her or walk into her office become the best versions of themselves through training, coaching, and mentoring.

Tanya graduated from Southern Illinois University - Carbondale with a degree in Workforce Education and Development. She has a graduate's degree in Organizational Leadership from Lewis University in Romeoville, Illinois focusing on Training and Development. She also has a postgraduate certificate in Human Resource Management from Keller Graduate School of Management, Downers Grove, Illinois. She is also a graduate from the Partnership for Public Service – Excellence in Government Fellows Program.

Tanya has served as a certified coach, mentor, master trainer, and her focus is to always leave the person she encountered via classroom, chat, or call, in a better place - feeling valued, seen, and heard. Tanya's inaugural book, *One Step At A Time – A Motivational Conversation*, is her way to give back to those who seek a path

One Step At A Time

forward professionally and personally because motivation and encouragement gives life and life more abundantly.

"It always seems impossible until it's done."

Nelson Mandela

One Step At A Time

TRH-Enterprises

One Step At A Time

Made in the USA
Monee, IL
21 July 2025

21576233R00056